# A DAY WITH A
# RACING  DRIVER

A DAY IN THE LIFE

# A DAY WITH A RACING DRIVER

Graham Rickard

# Other titles in this series

First published in 1980 by
Wayland Publishers Limited
49 Lansdowne Place, Hove
East Sussex, BN3 1HF, England

ISBN 0 85340 792 4

Typeset by Computacomp (UK) Ltd, Fort William, Scotland
Printed and bound in the United Kingdom by
W. & J. Mackay Ltd

# 1. This is Jochen. He is a racing driver.

*'Formula' racing defines the engine capacity, size of the car, and so on. A Formula One car has a maximum engine capacity of 3 litres, or 1.5 litres supercharged. The car must be a single-seater, and there are also regulations about the width of the car and its height above the ground.*

This is Jochen Mass, one of the world's top racing drivers. He first became interested in motor racing about fifteen years ago. Since then, he has driven many different kinds of racing cars. Jochen became a Formula One driver in 1973, and has driven in almost 100 Grand Prix races.

## 2. Jochen is in Madrid for the Grand Prix.

We join Jochen at Jarama race track near Madrid, the capital of Spain. Today is the second practice day, leading up to tomorrow's Spanish Grand Prix.

There are about fifteen Formula One teams in the world, and Jochen drives for the Arrows team. At the track, Jochen meets the team's chief executive, Jackie Oliver, and its other driver – Riccardo Patrese. They talk about the day's busy programme.

*A Grand Prix is the most important international race in a country's racing year. It is usually a Formula One World Championship event.*

# 3. The mechanics work on his car.

Meanwhile, the team's mechanics are working hard. They are adding finishing touches to the cars.

'We always take three cars to each race,' says Jochen, 'so that we have a spare in case one is badly damaged.'

As the cars sit in the hot Spanish sun, each one has a sunshade over the driver's cockpit to stop it from getting too hot.

## 4. The co-designer checks an aerofoil.

Dave Wass is the Arrows' co-designer as well as development engineer. He checks the angle of the rear aerofoil with one of the mechanics. The aerofoil is adjustable. It helps to keep the back wheels of the car firmly on the ground, in the same way as an aircraft wing keeps a plane in the air.

*Aerofoils are designed to stop the car lifting off the ground at high speeds. They usually consist of a wing on each side of the nose-cone, and a larger wing mounted above the rear wheels. An aerofoil is sometimes called a spoiler.*

## 5. The car's wings are protected by tape.

Special adhesive tape is stuck on to the front edges of the cars' smaller front wings. This protects the paintwork from flying gravel and stones. Different-coloured tape is used on each car, to help the team distinguish between Jochen and Riccardo as they speed past on the track.

## 6. Jochen waits in the transporter lorry.

Jochen has changed into his driving suit. He stands in the doorway of the team's transporter lorry, waiting to do his morning practice laps.

The transporter is used to carry the three cars to and from the race. It is also used as a changing-room for the drivers, and an office for the manager and designer. It contains all the spare parts for the cars, including whole replacement engines.

# 7. The co-designer makes notes.

*In the Arrows' A3 racer, the engine holds the whole car together. The engine, gearbox and rear aerofoil are held to the light chassis by only four bolts.*

Dave Wass makes a careful record of all the car's details. These include the size and type of tyres, wheel base, spring pressure, and gear ratio. Later these records will be used for further tests.

The Arrows team is famous for its advanced design work. They are constantly working on and adjusting the cars. This gives them an average speed increase of about one second per lap each year – and a second can be vital in racing!

# 8. Jochen signs an autograph.

On his way to the track, Jochen stops to sign an autograph for a fan. His racing suit is fireproof, and carries his name and blood-group in case he has an accident and needs a blood transfusion.

Jochen admits that motor racing is a dangerous sport, but adds: 'You accept it as a part of the sport, and try not to think about it too much.'

# 9. He enters the driver's cockpit.

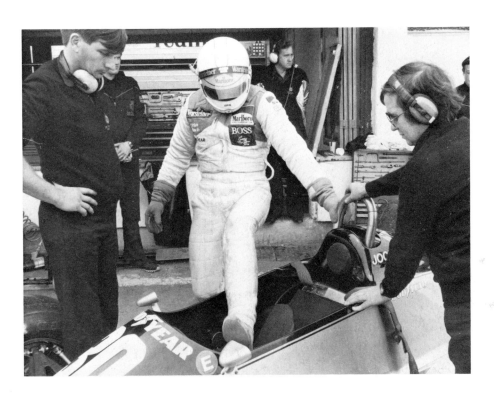

*The pits are an area beside the track, where cars can be worked on during a race. A pit-lane leads directly from the track to the pits.*

The car is now ready, and the team is waiting in the pit-lane. Jochen puts on his crash helmet and gloves, and the mechanics help him into the car.

The mechanics worked until late last night, and started again early this morning. They are anxious to see how the car performs on the race track. As Jochen says, 'A driver depends completely on his mechanics.'

## 10. Jochen is strapped into the car.

The mechanics strap Jochen firmly into the cockpit of the car. Jochen is larger than most racing drivers, and it is a tight fit. His legs rest on the metal bottom of the car, just two inches above the ground.

'It is important to be well strapped in,' says Jochen. 'When the car turns corners at high speed, my body weight increases to three times its normal weight.'

# 11. His helmet gives him protection.

*Jochen's helmet also has a built-in intercom system, so that he can talk to members of the team without removing his helmet (see Picture 16).*

Jochen's helmet is specially designed for motor racing. It is made in two halves, which are released at the touch of a button. The car has no windscreen to protect his face, but the helmet's transparent visor keeps the dust and rain out of his eyes.

If Jochen should become thirsty during a long race, he can press a switch in the cockpit which will release a spurt of glucose and water through a tube in the helmet.

## 12. The car is started by a mechanic.

One of the mechanics starts the car with a blast of compressed air from a large cylinder. The same cylinder is used to pump up the tyres. It also drives several tools, including the drill which removes the wheel nuts. Jochen has a small air-bottle in the car, in case he has to start the car himself.

# 13. Jochen begins his practice laps.

Jochen roars down the pit-lane towards the race track. A marshal waves a green flag to show that the track is clear. Jochen accelerates towards the first corner at the end of the straight.

Ahead of him lie several long sweeping bends, hairpin corners, and a hill. This is a track which will test the drivers' skill to the utmost. But Jochen has happy memories of Jarama – he won the Spanish Grand Prix here in 1975.

## 14. Jochen drives down the straight.

At the end of his first practice lap, Jochen races past the pits at over 270 k/h. This practice is not being timed, but the drivers push their cars to the limit. They hope to discover any faults or weaknesses in the car, before the qualifying laps this afternoon.

## 15. The car's tyres are checked in the pits.

*Formula One cars must have uncovered wheels. Because the engine drives the rear wheels, the largest wheels and tyres are at the back of the car to give it a better grip on the road.*

After several laps, Jochen pulls into the pits. His car tyres are already so hot that the air inside them has expanded and they have too much pressure. The mechanics release some of the pressure, while each tyre has its temperature measured.

The tyres are made of a special rubber which becomes sticky when warm, and helps the car to 'hold' the road. 'After one lap,' says a mechanic, 'the tyres are almost like chewing-gum.'

## 16. Jochen talks to the co-designer.

Dave Wass plugs his headset into a socket on the car. This allows him and Jochen to hear each other over the incredible noise of the race track. Dave has Jochen's lap times noted on his clipboard.

Dave and Jochen discuss what improvements can be made to the car.

# 17. The mechanics check the car.

*Each car has its own team of highly skilled mechanics. They try to make sure that the car gives a perfect performance, to match the driver's skill.*

The mechanics have set to work on Riccardo's car. They remove the light fibre-glass shell, and check all the important mechanical parts. Each mechanic is responsible for a different part of the car, and they all work very fast.

What is the thrill of racing for a mechanic, who spends all of his time in the pits? 'This is the height of the art ... It is our race, and our skill that counts, as much as the driver's,' they say.

## 18. Riccardo joins Jochen in the pits.

The mechanics push Riccardo's car to join Jochen in the pit-lane. Each Formula One team has a different colour – like football teams – and the Arrows' cars are mainly a glossy gold with black markings.

With its pointed nose cone and gleaming paintwork, the Arrows 'A3' model looks even more like an aeroplane or rocket than the other cars.

A marshal blows a whistle to clear the pit-lane, and Jochen's car speeds on to the track. Jochen wants to make the most of the hour-and-a-half practice session, by driving as many laps as he can. This will test the car thoroughly, and also allow Jochen to memorize every part of the twisting, up-and-down Jarama circuit.

This practice is not timed officially, but Jackie Oliver times all the cars from the track barrier. He presses a button every time a car roars past him. His computer timing machine then gives a read-out of the driver's speed for each lap.

*Off the track, an important part of Jackie's work is to find sponsors to provide the money needed to keep the team racing. Warsteiner, a German brewery, provides most of the Arrows' money. In return, their name is displayed prominently on the cars.*

# 21. The practice is over.

After a few more laps, the practice finishes. The drivers now return to the pits to discuss their laps with the designers and engineers. Jochen is hot, so he takes off the top of his driving suit.

Dave Wass records the details of the cars' performances. Jochen and Riccardo discuss what gear ratios would be best suited to the track.

## 22. The mechanics set to work again.

The drivers go to eat and rest, but there is still plenty of work for the mechanics to do. The cars are stripped down yet again. Springs and gears are changed, and an oil leak on Riccardo's car is fixed.

## 23. The car's cockpit is very small.

The cockpit of Jochen's car is very small. On the tiny dashboard, there are several dials which measure the engine speed, fuel pressure and water temperature. But, unlike an ordinary vehicle, Jochen's car has no speedometer.

The gear stick is to the right of the small steering wheel. Above the gearstick is an emergency switch, which turns on the fire extinguisher and supplies oxygen to Jochen's helmet.

## 24. The mechanics inspect the brakes.

Riccardo's mechanics are looking at the brakes on his car. Before a race or practice, the brakes are dabbed with special paints of different colours. At certain temperatures each colour disappears, which provides a useful record of the car's braking performance. In hot climates, such as here in Madrid, overheating brakes can be a big problem.

## 25. Spare parts are kept in the lorry.

The mechanics return often to the transporter lorry for spare parts. In their factory at Milton Keynes, the Arrows staff make almost every part for these cars, down to the last nut and bolt.

Most of the parts are made of special lightweight materials. These materials are very expensive – just one wheel rim can cost hundreds of pounds.

## 26. More vehicles arrive at the track.

More and more vehicles are arriving in the competitors' compound outside the race track. The unique atmosphere of the Grand Prix is beginning to build up.

'It's just like a big travelling circus, really,' says Jackie Oliver. Grand Prix races attract huge crowds in every country.

## 27. Jochen prepares for the timed practice.

*The grid is the area where cars line up in their starting positions for a race. The positions are arranged so that no car is directly behind the one in front of it.*

Jochen arrives back at the race track, and chats to Jackie Oliver and Doug Simpson, his chief mechanic.

Jochen is keen to do well in this afternoon's timed qualifying practice. His position on the starting grid for the Grand Prix will depend on his fastest single lap over the last two days.

## 28. The fuel tank is topped up.

Jochen sits in his car waiting to enter the track. The mechanics top up his fuel tank, which is directly behind his head. The tank holds well over 180 litres of petrol, which is a special five-star fuel.

The mechanics only put in as much petrol as they think Jochen will need – about 45 litres. The cars consume about 4.5 litres of petrol about every 8 kilometres, which is about three laps of the track.

# 29. The mechanics check their tools.

The mechanics use the last few minutes to tidy up the pits and arrange their boxes of tools. Good organization is very important in the pits, where everything is designed for speed. If a driver has to make a pit-stop during the race, the Arrow mechanics can change all four tyres and have the car back on the track in less than twenty seconds!

## 30. Jochen starts his qualifying laps.

Everything is ready, and Jochen's car shoots down the pit-lane. He then drives on to the track to begin his qualifying laps. His chances in the Grand Prix could be decided by this timed practice. A driver who starts the race near the front of the grid has a definite advantage.

# 31. The cars are timed by a computer.

The computerized timing equipment is in a special tower at the side of the track. Each car is fitted with a miniature radio transmitter which gives out a signal of a certain frequency. As the cars pass the timing tower, this signal is picked up and the drivers' lap times are measured to within a thousandth of a second.

## 32. Jochen is shown signboard.

As the drivers speed down the straight, the mechanics hold up signboards. These signals inform each driver of the number of his lap and the speed he has reached. They can also be used to remind the drivers to do things such as switch off their electric fuel pumps.

# 33. Jochen arrives back in the pit-lane.

Jochen pulls into the pit-lane to wait for the results of the practice. He and Riccardo were lucky enough to have a trouble-free run. Their only pit-stops were to take the tyre temperatures and release some of the air pressure. The cars had no mechanical problems at all.

This fact reflects the skill of both the designers and the mechanics. Jochen says proudly, 'We've finished more races this season than any other team.'

## 34. A reporter talks to the drivers.

Jochen and Riccardo sit beside the track and talk to a reporter. A Grand Prix always makes the headlines all over the world, and the Jarama track is already swarming with journalists and photographers.

# 35. Jochen visits the team's motor home.

Jochen walks out into the compound and goes to the Arrows' 'hospitality home'. All the teams have an area like this in the compound, where guests and journalists can go to relax during the breaks.

Jochen talks to Manfred Oettinger, who looks after the team's motor home and supplies them with food and drink.

## 36. Jochen listens to the time results.

The results of the timed practice come over the loudspeaker. Jochen changes out of his driving suit and sits outside the motor home to read the time-sheet. He finds that he will be in fourteenth place on the starting grid. Jochen's lap time was only two seconds slower than that of the fastest driver, Jacques Lafitte. Lafitte is now the favourite in the race.

## 37. Riccardo drives Jochen to the hotel.

Riccardo drives Jochen back to their hotel, where they both look forward to an early night. They want to be at their best for tomorrow's race. Riccardo was slightly faster in practice than Jochen, and will start the race in eleventh place.

After talking about the race, they turn to other subjects. When he is not driving, Jochen enjoys anything to do with water, 'especially sailing and diving'.

## 38. The mechanics continue working.

The drivers have finished their day, but the mechanics have many hours' work ahead of them. The cars are completely stripped down again, and work commences on the engine.

Afterwards, the mechanics check every part of the car as they put it back together. The most vital parts are replaced with spares. They don't want to leave anything to chance for tomorrow's race.

# **39.** Jochen gets dressed for the race.

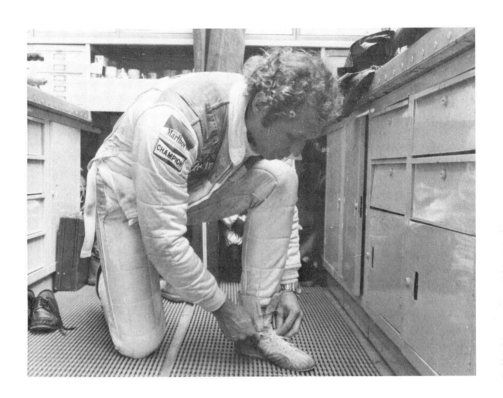

Jochen arrives back at the track early the next morning, and changes into his racing suit. His canvas boots are specially designed for racing. They have a reinforced heel, and a thin leather sole which allows him to feel the car's foot-pedals easily. Like the rest of his racing suit, the boots are fireproof.

## 40. Choosing tyres for the cars.

Alun Rees, the manager of the team, is supervising the choice of tyres. The stacks of tyres all have coded numbers chalked on them to show their size and type. Over this weekend, the team will use twenty sets of tyres.

The sun is already scorching hot. The team decides to use larger tyres than usual, to improve the car's road-holding ability.

# 41. Jochen waits to do his warm-up laps.

Before the afternoon's race, there is a half-hour warm-up. This will give the drivers a chance to test the cars, and to try out any last-minute changes which have been made.

Jochen climbs into the cockpit, and sits waiting for the all-clear. The crowds have begun to arrive, and the grandstand overlooking the track is gradually filling.

## 42. The mechanics fix a broken part.

The warm-up is soon over, but Jochen is not happy with his car. 'It isn't pulling away properly from the corners,' he tells the designers.

The mechanics set to work immediately, and soon find the cause of the problem. They fix it at once, and the whole car is checked thoroughly yet again.

# 43. Jochen talks to another driver.

The Spanish sun is now at its hottest, and Jochen pulls down the top half of his racing suit. Outside the pits, he meets Eddie Cheever, a young American driver who races for the Osella team. Jochen and Eddie are good friends, although they have raced against each other many times.

They compare their reactions to the Jarama track. It is the first time that Eddie has raced here, but he did well in practice and will be in tenth place on the starting grid.

## 44. Jochen puts on his racing helmet.

Jochen only has time for a brief rest before the loudspeakers announce that the race is about to start.

Jochen is relaxed and cheerful as he puts on his helmet. The mechanics have tidied up the pits, and are ready to handle any emergency during the race.

# 45. He leaves the car on the dummy grid.

*The dummy grid is an area behind the starting grid for the race. The cars assemble here and start their engines, before moving forward to the proper race grid.*

Jochen makes one lap of the track to warm up the car's engine. He then stops on a 'dummy grid' in front of the pits, and switches off. The mechanics have five minutes for any final adjustments to the cars, before the engines are started again.

It is so hot that Jochen and Riccardo get out of their cars. Once again, a sunshade is put over the cockpit to keep it cool.

## 46. The start of the race.

At last the track has been cleared. The drivers now drive one slow lap before stopping in their correct positions on the race grid – but this time they leave their engines running.

The drivers keep their eye on a light at the side of the track. When it changes from red to green, the race begins.

# 47. Thousands of spectators cheer.

The dramatic start to the race is watched by 70,000 spectators. They stand and cheer as their heroes flash past.

At this stage it could be anybody's race, for there is a long way to go. The track is over 3 kilometres long, and the drivers must do eighty laps or a total of about 272 kilometres.

## 48. Jochen moves into ninth place.

By the end of the thirty-fifth lap, the favourite, Jacques Lafitte, is just behind the Argentinian driver Carlos Reutemann. But Lafitte collides with the Spaniard, Emilio de Villota. The first three cars are involved in a spectacular crash. No one is hurt, but the leaders are out of the race.

Jochen seems relaxed and confident as he chases his team-mate round a corner.

# 49. Riccardo makes a pit-stop.

Riccardo is now forced to make a pit-stop. Smoke is pouring from his brakes, and the brake pedal has gone soft.

The mechanics work feverishly on the car. Within five minutes Riccardo is back in the race, but he will find it hard to make up the lost time.

Meanwhile Jochen has been driving well, and is now in fifth place.

## 50. Jochen finishes just behind the leader.

Now two of the leading cars are forced to retire with gearbox problems. Jochen is able to overtake the next driver on an inside corner.

On the sixty-sixth lap, a wheel falls off the leader's car, and Jochen has moved into second place. He crosses the finishing line only fifty seconds behind the winner. Out of the twenty-two starters in the race, only six cars crossed the finishing line.

# 51. The winners receive their prizes.

The crowd cheers as the first three drivers stand on the winner's rostrum for the presentation ceremony. Jochen receives a laurel wreath, a silver cup and a jeroboam of champagne. He will also gain a well-deserved six points in the World Championship Table.

## 52. The team congratulates Jochen.

Jochen fights his way back through the crowd of waiting fans, reporters and TV cameras. When he reaches the pits, the whole team is there waiting to congratulate him.

'How do you feel?'

'Great relief,' says Jochen. 'I was lucky.' He gives the bottle of champagne to the mechanics to say 'thank you'.

## 53. The cars are loaded on to the lorry.

Back at the pits, the mechanics begin to load the cars on to the transporter lorry, ready for the long drive back to England. They are very pleased that their hard work has paid off, and that Jochen's car did not let him down.

Once the cars have arrived back at the factory, the process will begin all over again. The cars will be stripped down, modified and rebuilt in time for the next race.

## 54. Jochen says goodbye.

John and Jackie shake hands as they say goodbye. They arrange to meet in England for the next track-test of the Arrows A3.

Jochen will fly home to have a few days off before the cars arrive. Then, within the next few weeks, he will be driving in yet another Grand Prix.

# Books to read

If you want to learn more about racing drivers, and motor racing in general, you may enjoy reading these books:

*Motor-racing* (Macdonald Focus on Sport series)

*The Observer's Book of Motor Sport* by Graham Macbeth (Warne)

*Motor Racing in Colour* by Doug Nye (Blandford)

*All about Motor Sport* by Nick Brittan (W. H. Allen)

*Guide to Racing Cars* by N. Roebuck (Franklyn Watts)

*Great Racing Drivers* by Doug Nye (Hamlyn)

*The Facts about a Grand Prix Team* by Barrie Gill (Deutsch)

*Grand Prix — The Know-how of Racing and Racing Cars* by Barry Rowe (Collins)

*Formula One* by Sven Zettergren (World's Work)

The author would like to thank

Jochen Mass
Jackie Oliver
Arrows Racing Team Ltd